The Lies *YOU* Tell...

A 21 Day Affirmation Journey

Back to Your Truth

Tanefa S. Wallace

About the Author

Tanefa Wallace is a Christian, mother, author and a teacher, first and foremost. She is also a Reiki master Practitioner and founder of Soul On Purpose, where she seeks to assist women in becoming their best self through life coaching, therapy and reiki.

Tanefa studied with Iyanla Vanzant in her Spiritual Life Coaching Certification Program for Inner Visions and Empowerment for Women at the beginning of her journey to wholeness and what she learned has guided her thus far. Affirmation, meditation and prayer are at the center of this book and have been integral to her personal practice as well as what she suggests to others seeking their center and their truth.

She lives in Baltimore MD with her two children, teaching, loving and living life.

**The Write Way
Baltimore, MD 21217
Manufactured in the United States of America
First Print**

*Library of Congress Number: 2017903422
ISBN: 978-0-692-85440-2
ISBN 10: 0692854401*

Reviews For T.S. Wallace's
First Novel

The Wayward Wife

"It's been a long time since I read an entire book in one day.... Especially a fictional work of art but the "The Wayward Wife" is the BOMB!!! It's so well written and I got so wrapped up in the characters and the story that I just had to finish it. The emotional suspense was overwhelming! I cannot say enough that this is a great read, especially for the ladies!! Colorful, moving and electrifying, it invites deep introspection on many women's approach to creating, maintaining, and healing relationships with self, friends, family and men. The characters are so real and multi-dimensional that it becomes easy for each of us to see part of ourselves in the characters in this work of art." – Ritta B.

"I loved this book! It's funny how you see yourself reflected in some characters, and wish you had the cajones to do what they do! T. Wallace is one of my new favorite authors. The way she switched POV's reminds me of Terry McMillan; you never get the characters confused and they keep the same voice throughout the novel. Without giving anything away, I can't wait to see what Neene is going to do now..." – Roslyn B.

"Read the book!!!!!!! Love love loved it!!!! Great thought provoking storyline with a message of forgiveness and redemption! Had me tearing up at a certain pivotal moment which I will not elaborate on as I don't want to give up too much. I highly recommend The Wayward Wife!!!!" – Anonymous Reader

"This book starts out with a fast pace that never lets up and keeps you turning pages. Wallace deftly weaves in backstories for her characters that give you a rich, long sense of history and how all of her characters fit together - and where they grew apart. The characters felt complex and I was genuinely rooting for the book's heroine, despite (or because of) her flaws. This is a great beach read! (although you may find yourself publicly blushing during some of the very well developed sex scenes ;) Read this before it becomes a movie!" – Maggie Master

"This book is outstanding! A serious page turner. I finished it in 3 days!!! A must read!" – Ann Petry

"Amazing read. This book was so exciting it kept me wanting to know what was next. The characters were relatable and omg the cliffhanger there has to be a sequel." – Anonymous Reader

This book is dedicated to women who speak over theirs and others lives without thought to the power of their word.

So is my word that goes out from my mouth: It will not return to me empty, but will accomplish what I desire and achieve the purpose for which I sent it. – Isaiah 55:11

In the beginning was the Word, and the Word was with God, and the Word was God. – John 1:1

Your word is a lamp for my feet, a light on my path – Psalm 119:105

Introduction

This book started with a dream that woke me up still talking! In the dream, I was involved in an argument with the enemy of mankind. I do not say that lightly. There was a force trying to convince me that I was unable to be successful and that I would fail at whatever I put my hand to! I rebuked that spirit quickly and began to say what you have on the pages to follow.

I realized in the process of writing this book, that we all have heard these kinds of words, either from ourselves or someone else. Words that discourage us and make us feel like we can't make it. Therefore, we all need the words to say to fight back! What better words than those from the *Word* to combat negativity? None, other than your own words for we know that the tongue can be used to build or destroy, to kill or bring forth life. Using your words to uplift and affirm yourself is the best defense and when coupled with scripture, you will be unstoppable!

A great way to distance yourself from the pain others cause with their words and actions, is to stop taking what people do and say to you personally. In addition, forgiving them and loving them despite their behavior is key, as is knowing that you may have to distance yourself from them if they are unwilling or unable to change.

When the voice you hear saying hurtful or undermining words is masked as your own, the same thing applies. You have to forgive yourself for feeling, saying and thinking negative things about yourself. It stops you from loving and respecting yourself when you don't forgive yourself for making mistakes. Plus, you can't distance yourself from yourself, although so many people try with drugs, alcohol and other obsessions, but that is another topic altogether.

So, How Do I Use This Book?

1. Look in the table of contents for the lie you are facing or that resonates with you, or even a close enough proxy of it.

2. Read my thought process of that lie's origin and/or how it has manifested within my life.

3. Then read the affirmations and scriptures to yourself and post them somewhere you can see and read daily before you start your day. For example, a bathroom mirror, entryway mirror, you can also get it nicely framed and add it to your décor.

4. If possible memorize the affirmation and/or scripture. Or use the notes page to create your own affirmation to reprogram your mind from believing the lie and follow the same process of reading and memorizing your own affirmations!

This process of repeating the affirmation and/or scripture must be repeated in some form for at least 21 days to form a habit, and 90 days to change your life!

Here are a few ways to get them to stick:

- Repeat once daily (like a vitamin!)

- Repeat up to 3 times a day at intervals

- If you have varying ones that you want to use, you can set an alert on your phone with your affirmations at odd hours of the day

- You can also repeat one of them multiple times in one sitting until the lie dissipates from your mind and these new thought patterns take its place (similar to a mantra)

This simple, yet so very effective way to handle negativity from others and myself is the basis of my emotional freedom. I broke down all the lies I told and those told to me, to expose the truths that freed me...

Table of Contents

You're Ugly!

What exactly is ugly anyway? Am I supposed to fit into your definition of beauty or be who I am as God designed me to be? I think the latter and not the former.

Your lips are too *big*. I was made with these lips to soothe my children's fears and my man's pains. Your butt is too high, too round, too bodacious... Well, ma'am, sir, I am fearfully and wonderfully made. My behind is a blessing and allows me to sit perched like a queen and everywhere I squat, a throne. No, I am not Eurocentric in my presentation and I won't be even if my hair is straightened... It's impossible for me to be other than who I am, and in that – I am beautiful.

Plus, as my mother always said, "Ugly is, as ugly does." The prettiest face can harbor the nastiest attitude and a spirit filled with self-hate. This made me as a young person focus on people's actions and their mannerisms more than what they looked like. It's what you do that makes you who you are, not what you look like anyway. Besides, when you are beautiful inside, you are able to astound people and they are able to see you as you truly are – exquisitely and wonderfully made.

Affirmation

I am happy, I am love, I am me, and I am beautiful.

I am perfect in my imperfections.

Scripture

Solomon 4:7 You are altogether beautiful, my love; there is no flaw in you.

Notes

_____

_____

_____

_____

_____

_____

_____

_____

_____

_____

_____

_____

_____

_____

_____

_____

You're Stupid!

Intelligence is personal. We are all intelligent in our own ways. We have been taught to think of intelligence as a linear thing that only responds to IQ tests and standardized exams, but genius is something that cannot be measured by those antiquated means. They thought Einstein was mentally retarded! How can I allow anyone to make me think I am not as smart as I should be? I am artistic, easily excited about new ideas, and the way I learn may not be the way you test.

Emotional intelligence, number sense, kinesthetic acumen and reading and writing ability are ways to be smart, not the only ways. For instance, my son has a learning disability, but he is a musical genius. He can learn songs, lyrics and pitch/tone within minutes. He can play the piano to the radio. Does he get perfect grades? No. Does that make him stupid? No. It means to me that he is unable to be a student in the way that the system he is currently working under requires. Can he read? Above grade level and does so voraciously. Am I worried? No. His purpose is his alone and perhaps he will not need traditional schooling to perform it.

Be who God made you to be. Your smart is yours alone.

Affirmation

God has made me intelligent in ways to fulfill my purpose.

Scripture

Exodus 31:3 ...and I have filled him (*her*) with the Spirit of God, with wisdom, with understanding, with knowledge and with all kinds of skills...

Notes

You Can't …!

I have been told I can't do a number of things in my life. *"You can't go back to school." "You can't move to another state with a toddler on your own." "You can't write a book."* I have also told myself, *"You can't find another job." "You can't pass that test."*

Well, I have done *all of these things and more* and although I can't say it was easy to do any of them, I can say that it was *worth it!* Most things you (or others) feel you can't do are based in fear. Your fear of the unknown, fear of what you've never done or seen done before, or even your fear of succeeding in an area of your life that has been for so long unexplored or left dormant will cripple and silence your ability to CAN.

Sometimes the people who say these things to you are also afraid. They are afraid that you will evolve and have no room for them in your evolution. They are afraid that you will surpass them in knowledge or in the field you share. They are afraid of losing you as a friend, sister, husband or wife. Usually, it's the person closest to you, or even yourself saying, "You can't…!"

But God says you *can.* If you go with what God says and follow the path He sets before you, there is nothing you can't do.

Affirmation

I am able.

I can do anything that I believe I can and am willing to work on and toward.

Scripture

Philippians 4:13 I can do all this through Him who gives me strength.

Notes

_____

_____

_____

_____

_____

_____

_____

_____

_____

_____

_____

_____

_____

_____

_____

_____

_____

Who Do You Think You Are?
(Implying that you aren't anyone at all...)

When confronted with this attitude or even this actual question, two questions come to mind, *"Who do you think I'm not?" And "Who do you think you're not?"*

Honestly, we are all evolving into our gifts and purpose and who I am may shift, but in this instance the question of who you are is more insidious in nature. Its implication is that you don't qualify to behave the way you are acting at any given moment! Being yourself does not require any prior authorization or pre-qualification. You are who you were made to be and you are growing into that person daily (if you are doing the work and paying attention).

Most of the time, I have encountered this attitude when I walk in authority and with purpose about a task that others *feel* they are more qualified to complete. Sometimes they are... On paper. But I know the way my life is set up is that sometimes I am not *qualified* on paper, but I am the perfect person for the job!

God has a way of qualifying those who are called to perform a certain task! Some people are not ready to acknowledge your ability, your presence or your gifts – Show them who you are!

Affirmation

I am a beloved child of The Most High.

Scripture

I John 3:1 See how great a love the Father has bestowed on us, that we would be called children of God; and such we are.

Notes

_____

_____

_____

_____

_____

_____

_____

_____

_____

_____

_____

_____

_____

_____

_____

No One Loves You &
No One Ever Will

I recall when an ex said these words to me. The pain was searing and the wound much deeper than I allowed him or even myself to acknowledge. I recently realized that he was projecting his own reality and pain onto me.

We can't make anyone love us, but we can show people how to treat us by the way we treat ourselves. Many of us mistakenly put our self-worth into the hands of other people who may or may not know how to handle this great responsibility, especially if we don't model what loving us looks like. Sometimes we grapple with the ability to forgive ourselves and treat ourselves in a way that makes others seem like they can join the party. Not so. Remember who you are and whose you are. Now, anyone in the space of my self-love must join in, or be repelled - it's really up to them.

Maybe your heart's been broken. Being heartbroken is a condition that is not diagnosable medically, but that doesn't lessen its effects. When your heart is broken, it can make you feel as if you aren't worthy of love or maybe just plain unlovable. What does that look like? It can look like depression. Withdrawal from affection. Bitterness. These things are manifestations of not being loved, but self-love and remembering that God loves you, is the cure!

Affirmation

"God loves me, adores me, watches over me, You are for me." - from Grace by Tasha Cobbs

I love and adore myself.

I am love and loved.

Scripture

1 John 4:16 ... to know and to believe the love that God has for us. God is love, and whoever abides in love abides in God, and God abides in him.

Notes

_____

_____

_____

_____

_____

_____

_____

_____

_____

_____

_____

_____

_____

_____

_____

_____

You're Weird

Being smart and unafraid to be myself seems weird in a world where everyone wants to fit in and be the same. I have always been different: sensitive, artistic, and introspective, but I was not always in the company of people who were similar or receptive to my being that way.

For a long time, I thought that being weird or a nerd or loving to read and ask a lot of questions made me a bad kind of different. Weird felt like a curse. As I grew older and wiser, I realized that all of those things made me not only who I was, but also set me apart from people who didn't think about or see things the way I do.

I realized that I am special. I am different and different was the best thing I could be in a world where conformity reigns. I have a dare for you. Embrace who you are and watch and see how those who are more like you than different, will be drawn to you.

Affirmation

I am unashamed of being different.

I love being one of a kind.

Scripture

I Peter 2:9 But ye are a chosen generation, a royal priesthood, an holy nation, a peculiar people...

Exodus 19:5 ...then ye shall be a peculiar treasure unto me above all people: for all the earth is mine

Notes

_____

_____

_____

_____

_____

_____

_____

_____

_____

_____

_____

_____

_____

_____

_____

_____

They're All Going to Laugh at You!

Let them laugh. I will never take what they do or say personally – I will be laughing too, being happy and content in my skin. Being, doing, loving and living.

When I wrote that title, I have to admit the refrain from Carrie's mother in that occult favorite rang in my mind. It was sad that her mother was the main one who detracted from her daughter's abilities (the one's closest to us.) and in doing so, twisted her into something that was an abomination. Just because she was afraid of her own daughter, she thought that no one would understand her and she would be ridiculed. Carrie could have had friends.

Don't you be afraid to make mistakes. Don't be afraid that people will laugh at you, because baby – sometimes they will! But it's okay, you just may have to join them!

Learning to laugh at yourself and learn from your mistakes is paramount to growing and becoming your best self. People who make mistakes are the ones who are actually doing things with their lives! I am always making mistakes, but never settling for second best from myself! I strive to be excellent and am getting better every day.

Affirmation

My ego and fear of ridicule will not stand in the way of my becoming my best self.

I am becoming my best self, daily.

I am learning to laugh at myself.

Scripture

Proverbs 17:22 A cheerful heart is good medicine, but a crushed spirit dries up the bones.

Notes

_____

_____

_____

_____

_____

_____

_____

_____

_____

_____

_____

_____

_____

_____

_____

_____

You Think You're All That.

Yup. You are completely correct. I am all that, with bag of Bon-Ton potato chips and a Pepsi too. Those who use this statement against you have a fear of them not being enough. They are living a comparative existence where they are measuring themselves and everyone else against an image of perfection that they have no hope of attaining. So who are you to shatter that image with your confident self?

Having confidence is great; having a big head is not. Confidence is knowing who you are and what you offer to any given situation is viable and important. Having a big-head is thinking you know it all and no one else knows anything at all or what they do know is irrelevant. Always be the former and not the latter as that is where your power lies.

The enemy is afraid of you knowing your power and will use any means to break you down. And sometimes so are you – afraid of what greatness lies within you. Don't allow people around you, your past or even your present, make you feel less than stellar.

Remember, God created you amongst all creation to be in His image and He is all of that!

Affirmation

I am all that; you are all that; we are ALL, "all that" as we are ALL created in the image of God.

Scripture

Genesis 1:27 So God created mankind in His own image, the in the image of God He created them; male and female He created them.

Notes

_____

_____

_____

_____

_____

_____

_____

_____

_____

_____

_____

_____

_____

_____

_____

_____

It's Impossible.

Sometimes the things we face seem insurmountable. Things like a cancer diagnosis or the passing of a loved one. Perhaps your debt is high and your pay is low and you have no idea of how you will pay it off. But anything can be done with patience, persistence, prayer, will power, and faith in God's desire for things to go well with you.

It's these same things that will send you either to a place to get centered and remember the promises of God or to a place of darkness where you get farther away from those same promises. If there is something that is supposed to happen, do all that you can do to make it come to pass and then wait on God. But wait on God in faith, not worry, because worry is an indication that you don't trust God to make things shift for you.

You have to have faith that you will make it happen! If you feel defeated – you will be. And walking around defeated will defeat your purpose for being here. We can't have that.

Affirmation

I am possible, therefore nothing is impossible.

Patience, persistence, prayer and will power will propel me toward fulfilling my dreams and reaching my goals.

Scripture

Matthew 19:26 But Jesus looked at them and said, "With man this is impossible, but with God all things are possible."

Jeremiah 29:11 For I know the plans I have for you," declares the Lord, "plans to prosper you and not to harm you, plans to give you hope and a future.

Notes

_____

_____

_____

_____

_____

_____

_____

_____

_____

_____

_____

_____

_____

_____

_____

_____

I'm Broke!

Saying these words aloud is prevalent in many communities and this is gonna take a bit of work to dismantle, so hold – this one will be a doozy!

Whatever you call yourself becomes what and who you are, which is why I cringe when I hear people say those words. Your self-talk becomes a self-fulfilling prophecy! Speak *life* to your finances and every other area of your life while you're at it! Although having little is and can be a reality, *how you think* about what you *do have* is key, as well as *what you do* with what you have. Your attitude and perspective about money, success and prosperity is more indicative of what you will ever be able to have than what you actually have in your bank account.

If you are afraid of money, either having it, because you never have and don't know what to do with it, or not having it and are afraid of lack, you will never be able to maintain or increase your financial status. ***What you focus on becomes your reality.*** If you focus on lacking, you will lack. If you focus on fear of squandering of what you do have, squandering is what will happen.

Contrarily, if you focus on being grateful for what you have and are prudent with it, but not afraid of what you have monetarily, it will grow.

Affirmation

I am open to accepting, receiving and utilizing all forms of abundance God (YHWH) and the Universe has to offer me.

I respect money and all forms of abundance.

I treat my abundance appropriately by keeping track of my spending and by saving.

Scripture

Romans 8:17a If we are His children, we are also God's heirs.

Proverbs 21:5 The plans of the diligent lead surely to plenty, but those of everyone who is hasty, surely to poverty.

Matthew 25:19-21 19 After a long time the master of those servants returned and settled accounts with them. 20 The man who had received five bags of gold brought the other five. 'Master,' he said, 'you entrusted me with five bags of gold. See, I have gained five more.' 21 "His master replied, 'Well done, good and faithful servant! You have been faithful with a few things; I will put you in charge of many things. Come and share your master's happiness!'

Notes

_____

_____

_____

_____

_____

_____

_____

_____

_____

_____

_____

_____

_____

_____

_____

_____

_____

I Can't Change.

I know you've heard the saying, "The only thing constant is change." We all have. The thing that's layered beneath that, the thing that people don't say aloud is, "I'm afraid of change." People don't say it because they know they can't stop change I guess, or maybe they feel like since they know they can't control it, it doesn't make sense to voice their fears. The problem then becomes their behavior. The silent resistance to change. What they do, say and act out is, "That's just the way I am." Or, "It's just the way I was taught." Or even, "My momma did it like that and so did her momma! It can't be that bad!" That attitude or the approach to change makes it all the more difficult for the inevitable change to take place. Oh and it's coming...

I had a friend from childhood, who hasn't changed much, confront me about my eating habits while at my house for dinner. We were having fish and she wanted to know where the meat was! I don't eat red meat or pork and haven't for at least 20 years plus and I explained to her that it was a hard change for me because I loved oxtails so much, but my health was just so much more important to me.

She was like, "I understand I guess, but I'm gonna eat my pork chops! Shoo! My momma ate pork chops, my grandmamma ate them too. Why wouldn't I!?" I wanted to say to her, "Your momma died of a heart attack after years of struggling with hypertension and your grandmother had a stroke from her high blood pressure," but I didn't. Maybe I should have, but in her mind she was doing what she knew, what was familiar and routine and what I was doing was foreign, strange and she wasn't about to change!

Sometimes it's our own fears and feelings of inadequacy, our unfamiliarity or our lack of preparedness for what's ahead, that leads us to tell ourselves this boldface lie. We have to know that new and different doesn't have to mean wrong and negative. Usually, it's for our betterment and even when change is hard, remember that you are not alone.

Affirmation

I am open to change as a doorway to better.

I can do and be different than what I have been shown and have learned.

Scripture

Isaiah 43:19 (KJV) Behold, I will do a new thing; now it shall spring forth; shall ye not know it? I will even make a way in the wilderness, and rivers in the desert.

Notes

This Page Left Intentionally Blank

Use as you wish to draw, muse without lines... Do you!

I'm Afraid.

Fear. This is no lie actually. I am frequently feeling trepidatious about a move I want to make, but I realize that fear is one of two emotions, that I can actually choose to feel. The other is love. Every other emotion is a branch from either of those trees. When I begin to feel the creep of apprehension, I stop and dissect it immediately and choose to feel differently. I change my perspective about what I face. I know intimately that fear will have you imagining the worst case scenario and breathing life into that instead of what good may come to you by having faith. I also know that whatever you think will happen, will. Whatever you focus on will become your perspective. Fear makes you doubt the love that God has for you and his plan for your life, whereas if you know you are loved, you can live without constraints or limitations.

Fear is the anti-love.

This is not to say that as humans we won't feel afraid. It's important to our survival as species to fear certain circumstances and to be able to discern when we are in trouble or danger. This fear is the lie we tell when we are unwilling to dig deeper past that protective response to unearth our triggers. This work is difficult, but needed so we don't wake up one day and find ourselves afraid of being ourselves, afraid of who we are not being acceptable, afraid of what we are capable of and can accomplish.

Affirmation

"Fear is for others." - Bruce Lee

I am filled with faith, light and love.

Scripture

Philippians 4:6 Do not be anxious or worried about anything, but in everything by prayer and petition with thanksgiving, continue to make your requests known to God.

2Timothy 1:7 For God did not give us a spirit of timidity, or cowardice or fear, but of power and of love and of a sound judgement and personal discipline.

Notes

_____

_____

_____

_____

_____

_____

_____

_____

_____

_____

_____

_____

_____

_____

_____

_____

_____

You Are Just Like _____
(Fill in the Blank)

Many times these words are uttered in frustration and the person stating this is remembering something that is not flattering about who they are likening you to. Do not be dismayed. You may very well be like the person in some form or fashion, but do not mistake it, you are an individual. I recall when my mother likened me to my absent father. I didn't know how to take initially. I was kind of happy to have some connection to him and even though she was mad at me, I was secretly happy that I was in some way just like him.

Sometimes wounds created by this statement can be deep and far reaching. If you resemble the absent parent in your life, or if your ways are similar to someone who has caused pain to the person speaking this lie to you, or you know this person to be a real jerk, be wary of accepting it. You are **not** *just like* anyone.

You have a particular mix of all the right things that have never existed before. You are your own kind of wonderful stardust shaped into a gift for humanity.

Affirmation

I am me as only I can be.

I am unlike anyone that has ever walked the face of the earth.

I am gifted in my own unique way.

Scripture

1 Peter 4:10 As each one has received a special gift, employ it in serving one another as good stewards of the manifold grace of God.

Notes

_____

_____

_____

_____

_____

_____

_____

_____

_____

_____

_____

_____

_____

_____

_____

_____

_____

I Can't Say No!

Saying no is hard at times. I will admit it is especially hard when you are in relationship with someone and want to say no desperately, but it just won't come out! When I say in relationship, I don't mean just the intimate kind with your husband, wife or significant other– I mean *all of them*. The relationships with your children, your siblings, your co-workers and yes, the one with your boss too, can all receive the answer no at any given time and place.

This lie is included because there are times we *need* to say no and we don't. We lie to ourselves about our ability to stand up for ourselves and our personal space. We allow ourselves to be pushed into places beyond our capacity at the moment and out of our place of feeling right within ourselves. Our inability to say no can leave us feeling angry, abused and used. But it's all our fault. Iyanla Vanzant recently referenced The Course in Miracles in an interview. She recounted where it says that when you give to others to the point where you sacrifice yourself, you make the other person a thief because they are stealing from you what you need for yourself and they don't even know it. What I have realized in my experience is that, we tend to then want to martyr ourselves and vilify them from stealing from us with resentment and anger they don't deserve, because they didn't know that we wanted to say no in the first place!

You can say no. No is a one-word sentence. It means, "I will not allow you to intrude on this space or time that I have reserved for something else or for myself." It means, "I am unable to comply with your request." Perhaps it may even be a temporary no, but it is still a no.

Boundaries and a need for acceptance are the main issues underlying why we don't say no. We feel like others are entitled to have access to our time, space and even our minds, sometimes to the expense of what we need to give ourselves. We fear that they won't love us, employ us, or be our friend anymore. To be in fear of the dissolution of any relationship because of our personal needs and boundaries is no way to live.

Let your no, be firm, and your yes, a resounding one.

Affirmation

I am able to set and enforce boundaries with love and self-respect.

My no, is no and my yes, yes.

Scripture

Exodus 18:14-23 Moses' father-in-law replied, "What you are doing is not good. You and these people who come to you will only wear yourselves out. The work is too heavy for you; you cannot handle it alone. Listen now to me and I will give you some advice, and may God be with you. You must be the people's representative before God and bring their disputes to him.

Galatians 6:5 For each will have to bear his own load.

Notes

_____

_____

_____

_____

_____

_____

_____

_____

_____

_____

_____

_____

_____

_____

_____

_____

This Page Left Intentionally Blank

Use as you wish to draw, muse without lines... Do you!

I Never Have Enough

Ever have that gnawing feeling that you aren't going to have enough of something; money, food, time or even love? Maybe the conscious thought or feeling went unnoticed, but actions it spurred are clear. The miserly spending, not money consciousness and budgeting, but truly miserly – which has its word roots in miserable, meaning that what you are doing is not coming from a place of happiness and integrity with money, but another place. A place steeped in fear. The fear of not having enough. The rushing about frantically, not really planning but panicking about how your time is being wasted or trying to do everything now because, well, you fear there won't be time later. Or maybe it's you at the cookout making plates upon plates to take home or taking leftovers from every event and it's not because you don't have food at home, or you don't feel like cooking dinner; it's because you feel compelled.

Thoughts of *never* having enough, is a *lack mindset*. Lack can be a pervasive motivator and it sometimes mimics determination and frugality, but how you know it's different is the way it feels. It feels shameful, or like you aren't a good person, or like you are anxious. Not as if you are accomplished or goal oriented, like you feel when you are budgeting and conscious of your time and intentions. Be aware of the underlying intentions!

Affirmation

I always have enough of all my needs.

My needs are always provided for right on time, every time.

Scripture

2 Corinthians 9:8 And God will generously provide all you need. Then you will always have everything you need and plenty left over to share with others.

Notes

_____

_____

_____

_____

_____

_____

_____

_____

_____

_____

_____

_____

_____

_____

_____

_____

_____

I Am Alone

I know. This doesn't seem like it can be a lie right? You may be sitting in a café, quite by yourself right now. Or even sitting on your couch with some popcorn and a soda, reading this like, "What is she talking about?" You know what I mean though, don't you? Even when we are *all by ourselves*, (and yes, I sang that song in my head a little as I typed that...) we are never truly alone in the universe.

Let's be honest; we may feel painfully lonely and ache for companionship, but in the end, we always have ourselves. Us and God or the universe (if that is what you call your higher power) are always present and because of that one fact, we are never truly alone.

Knowing that may not extinguish the pangs for company we may feel, but we can remedy that by treating ourselves like we are our own best thing. Sounds a little weird, doesn't it? But trust me, being alone is not a bad thing. Get to know who you are! What you like. Where you like to be and feel most yourself. Date you! Become your own best friend. Then, when someone else comes along, they see how you treat you, and will have to follow suit; because after all, you won't let anyone else treat you worse than you treat you – Right? Right. Being alone is the training ground for being with someone else and still being you.

Affirmation

I am my very best thing.

I am comfortable and enjoy doing things by myself.

I am never alone; I take God with me wherever I go.

Scripture

Joshua 1:9b Do not be frightened, and do not be dismayed, for the Lord your God is with you wherever you go.

Isaiah 41:10 fear not, for I am with you; be not dismayed, for I am your God...

Notes

I'm Too Busy To...

We are all scheduled to the edge of sleep and just too busy for so many things it seems... But let's look a little further into what is occupying this time we have, remembering that Oprah, Beyoncé and Michelle Obama, all have the same 24 hours in a day that we have, and see what's really happening.

Believe I am not saying in any way that you aren't busy. *We all are.* What I am asking is *how* are you spending your time? Are you doing things with your time that honor who you are and where you want to be mentally, physically, spiritually and emotionally? Then maybe you are too busy and need to cut some of that "busy-mess" out and get busy doing things like meditation, prayer, working out, goal setting, planning and executing.

Entertain me for a moment here; this was my self-talk around finding time to meditate, pray and do yoga daily. "I am too busy! Between being at work as a teacher, a full time mom of a 10 year-old and part-time mom of a semi-grown up away at college, a wig maker, Reiki practitioner and several other ventures, my head is spinning."
All of this busy-mess was exactly why I needed to be doing the meditation, prayer and yoga!

I had to do a serious look at how I was spending my waking hours and utilizing my calendaring process. Being too busy for what will keep me sane in the midst of all I am responsible for, was a serious problem! Bottom line, I had to find the time for the important things! Being and feeling centered and whole was, and still is a priority for me.

What are *your priorities*? Start there and find the time for the things that are *most* important. Never be too busy to do things for your well-being. That's surely a way to crash and burn.

Affirmation

I make time for the things that center my soul.

I am able to do all that I need to, in the time I have available.

Scripture

Luke 10:38-42 Now as they went on their way, Jesus entered a village. And a woman named Martha welcomed him into her house. And she had a sister called Mary, who sat at the Lord's feet and listened to his teaching. But Martha was distracted with much serving. And she went up to him and said, "Lord, do you not care that my sister has left me to serve alone? Tell her then to help me." But the Lord answered her, *"Martha, Martha, you are anxious and troubled about many things, but one thing is necessary.* ***Mary has chosen the good portion, which will not be taken away from her.***"

Ephesians 5:11 & 17 Don't waste your time on useless work, mere busywork, the barren pursuits of darkness... Don't live carelessly, unthinkingly. Make sure you understand what the Master wants.

Notes

_____

_____

_____

_____

_____

_____

_____

_____

_____

_____

_____

_____

_____

_____

_____

_____

_____

_____

This Page Left Intentionally Blank

Use as you wish to draw, muse without lines... Do you!

Dis Too Much or
I Can't
or I Cannot
(AKA - I Am Overwhelmed)

Long title for one lie huh? Yeah... I get it, but this is one I see and hear all of the time! And it frazzles my nerves. I even say it myself! When I feel like throwing everything into the air and fleeing to a deserted island, alone – this is what I say. I also say this when I see something someone else does or says that is just way over the top.

The thing is, I am and I can. In that moment, I am dealing with whatever has come my way and instead of facing it like the conqueror I am, I am dreading it or making it bigger than I am. Why? Especially when I know how powerful my words are and that my tongue is a powerful tool. It can build roadblocks or destroy any doubts I have about my ability to succeed and to deal with life.

I was listening to one of my favorite gospel songs, "I Won't Be Defeated" and it says, "...the situation don't defeat you!" The scriptures tell us that weapons will form but we have to remember that they will not prosper – we will.

Affirmation

I can handle all that life presents me.

I am fully equipped for all my challenges.

I am able and willing.

Scripture

Psalm 23:4 Yea, though I walk through the valley of the shadow of death, I will fear no evil: for thou art with me; thy rod and thy staff, they comfort me.

Psalm 91:7 A thousand may fall at your side,
And ten thousand at your right hand;
But it shall not come near you.

Notes

_____

_____

_____

_____

_____

_____

_____

_____

_____

_____

_____

_____

_____

_____

_____

_____

I Am Not Enough

This lie is insidious. I say this because it is an invisible lie. It doesn't manifest in ways that are obvious to it being the underlying issue. It's not like you are saying "I'm broke," and it's obvious because you don't have money. This lie speaks to how you treat yourself and allow others to treat you; it speaks to what you expect from life. It can be as simple as having low self-esteem and manifest in self-depreciating behavior where you can't even accept a compliment without criticizing yourself. Or as complicated as being in a relationship where you aren't fulfilled or supported, but staying in it because you don't know if anything better will ever come.

Feeling like you are not enough can lead to behavior that is self-defeating. For instance, I have wanted to write this book for a couple of years. I thought to myself, *"Who am I to give this message to people? Why would they listen to me? I am imperfect."* I am hardly what I would consider to have it *"all together,"* but in the writing of this book and the vetting of all of these lies, I realized that because the message came *through* me, I am enough.

I am capable and able to be a conduit for others and my own healing without being perfect because even in my imperfect state of being, I am enough. And so are you.

Affirmation

I am enough.

I am worthy of all God and the Universe has for me.

I honor myself and recognize my worth.

Scripture

Luke 12:6-7 Are not five sparrows sold for two pennies? And not one of them is forgotten before God. Why, even the hairs of your head are all numbered. Fear not; you are of more value than many sparrows.

Psalm 139:13-14 For you formed my inward parts; you knitted me together in my mother's womb. I praise you, for I am fearfully and wonderfully made.

Notes

_____

_____

_____

_____

_____

_____

_____

_____

_____

_____

_____

_____

_____

_____

_____

_____

You're Weak!

Well, being human is being prone to frailty, is it not? Weakness is a real thing! Whether in body or mind, sometimes being weak is appropriate. But when someone says that to you is that what they mean? Or are they using it as an accusation? Or as a put down? Are they saying that your will power is low and that you aren't able to stand up for yourself? Are they saying that you are spineless? How do you feel about that? Are you weak?

That is for you to determine. No one else. And when you are weak, it is not a condemnation. It's a statement of fact. And it is okay to be so, because it is fixable, although not in the way you would think. There is always a way to make weaknesses stronger. How? First is to acknowledge them for yourself and don't let anyone make you feel ashamed. We are all human and there is a certain beauty in our weaknesses.

Affirmation

I am strong enough.

There is strength in my weakness.

Scripture

2 Corinthians 12:9-10 But he said to me, "My grace is sufficient for you, for my power is made perfect in weakness." Therefore, I will boast all the more gladly about my weaknesses, so that Christ's power may rest on me. That is why, for Christ's sake, I delight in weaknesses, in insults, in hardships, in persecutions, in difficulties. For when I am weak, then I am strong.

Isaiah 40:29 He gives strength to the weary and increases the power of the weak.

Notes

_____

_____

_____

_____

_____

_____

_____

_____

_____

_____

_____

_____

_____

_____

_____

_____

I'm Okay

This is the one lie I say all of the time. I say it for so many reasons and most of the time, if I am honest with myself, it's a lie. I can be doing a myriad of things in the moments I say this lie to myself, but sometimes I don't want to do the work of being aware or in-tuned to how I am really feeling in that moment.

I also don't want to unload on anyone. That's a tough place to be, but as a reformed people pleaser, it's a real thing to not want to make anyone else feel uncomfortable, even if they love me and are genuinely interested in my emotional, mental and spiritual state of being. I have learned that we are not meant to live our lives hiding from our emotions or not sharing them, but we are meant for community and that requires vulnerability and a measure of openness reserved for those who love and care for us.

Above all of that, being okay is not even a great thing to be! It denotes mediocrity and I am far from mediocre. What about you?

I have begun to incorporate three different phrases into my lexicon that I use now instead of saying, "I'm okay." I will share those in a minute, but I want to be clear that sometimes I do feel, *just okay*. In those moments, I have begun to challenge myself to dig deeper, to make certain of the feelings that are lurking beneath the surface of my "middle of the road" presentation and explore them, so that I am living a more aware existence.

I also make sure to only speak what and where I want to be, and not where I am unless I feel the need to share with those who love and support me. I do this because words have life and I want them to be purposeful as they leave my lips.

Affirmations

I am blessed and highly favored.

I am wonderful.

I am doing well.

Scripture

John 16:33 I have told you these things, so that in me you may have peace. In this world you will have trouble. But take heart! I have overcome the world.

Notes

_____

_____

_____

_____

_____

_____

_____

_____

_____

_____

_____

_____

_____

_____

_____

_____

This Page Left Intentionally Blank

Use as you wish to draw, muse without lines... Do you!

Acknowledgments

First and foremost, I want to give thanks and honor to God for giving me the words to speak over myself the night I was awakened by that argument with the enemy! I am feisty, but when under attack, having the right weaponry is so important. *Babygirl got all the right weaponry!* (I couldn't help myself – if you know me, then you get it...) It is also important to note that the voice was extremely familiar to me, which is why I wanted to be sure that I looked at this from the perspective of the lies we tell ourselves along with the lies others may say to us.

I also need to acknowledge my children, Tihira and Joseph, as they are always integral to my creative process and bear the brunt of my hectic schedule and absent mindedness as it pertains to anything outside of writing! They are also inspirational, as writing this book made me focus keenly on all of our self-talk and helped us as a family to be more mindful. As my mother, Yasmin, used to say, *"Be mindful, even when your mind is full."* Her jewels of wisdom or *Yazisms*, as we call them are a large part of who I am and how I move through this life. She believed in speaking life into her children.

I also want to thank all of the people who have encouraged my gift, Walter Fredericks, Cole and Aisha Pew, my sisters, Karima, Danielle, Zakiya

(and bonus sister Deja), Nilajah Brown, Yusuf
Dashiell and hosts of others I cannot fathom to
name here, but who lifted and encouraged me when
giving up seemed easiest to do.

Love and thanks to you all!

For News and Information on
Upcoming Books and other Projects...

Website:
www.TanefaWallace.com

IG:
@TheWriteWayPub

Facebook:
www.Facebook.com/WriteWay

(

www.ingramcontent.com/pod-product-compliance
Lightning Source LLC
LaVergne TN
LVHW052034080426
835513LV00018B/2317